Frank
Chrissy Banks

smith|doorstop

the poetry business

Published 2021 by
Smith|Doorstop Books
The Poetry Business
Campo House,
54 Campo Lane,
Sheffield S1 2EG

Copyright © Chrissy Banks 2021
All Rights Reserved

ISBN 978-1-912196-83-8
Typeset by The Poetry Business
Printed by Biddles, Sheffield

Smith|Doorstop Books are a member of Inpress:
www.inpressbooks.co.uk

Distributed by NBN International, 1 Deltic Avenue,
Rooksley, Milton Keynes MK13 8LD

The Poetry Business gratefully acknowledges
the support of Arts Council England.

Contents

7	Frank
8	Ola
9	Whistle Down the Wind
10	What's the Matter, Christine Fox?
11	You Can Do Better Than That
12	At Castle Neroche
13	Fossil Beach
14	Young Again
16	Day Trip
17	Viewpoint
18	The Green
19	Cicada Love Song
20	At the Juliet House, Verona
21	Late, Alone
22	I'm Probably Wasting My Time and Yours
24	I'm on Page 3
25	when was ecstasy
27	Black Cat and Rabbit
28	Tales of the Poets
30	on not being william carlos williams
31	The Nearly Times
32	The Waves

frank (adjective)
honest, sincere, and telling the truth,
even when this might be awkward
or make other people uncomfortable

for Nigel

Frank

In that very southern university,
we were northern aliens, experiments
in academia, mad in love with literature,
first in the family to win a place.

Winter or summer, he shrugged thin arms
into a khaki parka. His hooked nose poked
from a face pale as bleached flour. He kissed me
once, in Anglo-Saxon, rough and slobbery.

Frank couldn't do with borrowed thought.
When he spat words straight from the seam,
hard and black, his tutors' eyes lit up.
He didn't give a toss if they agreed or not.

Analysing Hamlet *(he's fucking fucked)*,
evaluating Wordsworth *(that bloke wins first prize
fer turning kids off poetry)*, rattling off his own
deranged and genius critique of Hemingway,

he gobbed and scrawled himself a First.
The last I heard, he'd won a scholarship,
soared off to be Frank in New York, while I
wondered what it meant to *graduate*.

What I'm thinking now, too late, is this:
I could have learned a lot from Frank.

Ola

The music is way up loud and so is she,
just back from Ibiza where she danced all week.
Today in the gym it's Body Jam, Ola out front.
She swishes her palomino ponytail. *I've missed you
so much*, she swears to us all in warm,
Ukrainian vowels. Her skin shines
like butterscotch. Her electrics are all turned on:
smile sparking, whites of her green eyes
lit up. 'That Power' is pumping out and Ola
is spreading her arms as though she'd embrace us all.
I feel so good, she proclaims, skipping from side
to side, head thrown back to the ceiling.
Her hands smooth her body from neck
to thighs as she sways. *You don't have to do this*,
she smiles. But the slender girls, the new mothers,
the serious-muscled of either sex, the young
pensioners in the back row, one way or another
we all want what you have, Ola.
Turn! she says and we turn. *Spin!* she commands
and we spin. *Fly!* We're flying, we fly.
Ola, even your name is a whoop of joy.

Whistle Down the Wind

This was one of those Sixties films
set in the black and white North.
I knew the meaning of monochrome,
of dark-eyed, dark-haired,
hungry, unshaven men.

I was younger than Hayley Mills,
but I knew Jesus was dead, knew
he would never be back,
that no-one is ever saved
by a ghost, whatever they said.

The moonish faith those kids
offered to 'Jesus', a man
on the run. I imagined him
free for their sakes, but I wanted
to wrestle their certainty into the mud.

And I wanted to weep when they stole
for him, handed their souls to the liar.
Wanted to find some word or act,
when the police took him away,
to comfort them, to comfort myself.

What's the Matter, Christine Fox?

I'd never been asked that one before –
except as a slap or silencing sweet to suck.
This was more, *What grieves you so much?*

She spoke softly, no-one else near,
end of the Art class. Shocking to hear
my name, my full name spoken. Our eyes locked,
hers amber and wise. *What's the matter, Christine Fox?*
Nothing, I said and hid under my hair.

As I went off to English or French, I looked up
at a sky dark with crows over a wheat field aflame,
Van Gogh's tortured way to give words the slip.

What colour and shape are shame? And how to begin?
For so long, I'd buried so much. If it was anyone
it would be her – but I wasn't about to give in.

You Can Do Better Than That

Cathy, it's time you stopped
running around on the moors all day.
And drop that rough orphan boy
your dad brought home. He's a bad lot.

I know you think it's love,
but take it from me, it's not.
Don't think I'm too old to know about passion,
but it has to be tamed, or else you're stuffed!

A bright spark like you, why aren't you
at school, like other girls your age?
There's a whole world out there.
Get an education, get a job!

You're worth more than marriage
to any of that shower round here.
Make your own way. Don't be a slave
to some bullying brute. Don't be a fool

for a lad with the raging hots for you
but nothing between his ears.
Cathy, I know you're hormonal,
but you've got to calm down.

Stop running around on the moors
with that brooding boy, love,
or take it from me,
it's all going to end in tears.

At Castle Neroche

Along by the birches, into the pine forest,
the dog going doolally to be free, rounding up the children,
minding his flock in that leafy sphere.

It was as if we'd packed all our conflicts into a boat
and floated them off somewhere, so we could be here,
close, in the quiet woods.

Snowdrops, pine cones and puffballs, sinuous roots,
a phallic stinkhorn. Five of us moving together
among all that simply grows.

I found a berry like a ruby on the forest floor.
For a while, that small gem held us
in a ring of silence.

Fossil Beach

The cobbled shore at Kilve
twenty years ago.
Three stand together and look our way
each at that point in young life
when the future spreads out restless and wide as the sea
when every change hits
with the sting of salt spray
and people drop away
in the dip of a wave.

But the girl in orange sundress and trainers
seems never happier than this
between her two brothers, the pair posed
for an imaginary album cover
all elbows and angsty frowns.

Her lips part in a smile
one hand shielding her eyes
as if from a too painful light
one foot forward as though she might leave.
But she doesn't – not this day.

And the camera will not foreshadow
all that spins them apart
but fixes an imprint, an image
to last the span of their lives,
while the bones of an afternoon
are ghosted on memory's stone.

Young Again

As if they'd been waiting for us
    they appear

their black backs two wet rocks
    that have learnt to swim.

Show-offs, mother and baby
    snorting fountains that glide
buck
        and dip
play us
    with their vanishing acts

and *there!*
    re-appear upended
cleft tails raised till
    toppling

a weight of leather
    slaps against the ocean's skin.

Then the mother whale glides
    under the world of the boat

and we are young again
    bums up   leaning over the side

to witness the slow slide
    of her back
        emerging
and it keeps coming

    moment by moment
        mile by mile
like a planet
swimming itself
        through the birthing waters
back when time itself
    was a child.

Day Trip

It's a great day, she said,
for a visit to Clare Island.
Madness of course. The cold
was biting our cheeks and fingers
as we stood, hooded against the wind,
while smoky clouds gathered overhead.

But all that day on Clare Island,
as velvety rain softened
our hair and faces, and we knelt
to look at an orchid, or lifted binoculars
to a risen meadow pipit
on the path to the lighthouse,
her words sang out.

On our return, she asked how it was.
Lovely, we said. *We had a fine day.*
 Of course you did, of course.
 It's always a fine day on Clare Island.

Viewpoint

Some days,
a walk in the woods,
a look at the lake,

flashes a mirror
into another dimension,
dazzles me.

Then, I might almost
let myself think, *This
isn't everything.*

Today, rain muddies the track,
dribbles through trees.
The lake turns in on itself.

Someone else
may make a myth
or a slice of heaven from this

but that brown dog flying
between bank and water
is no more Pegasus

than the silver torso
of a downed birch
is a fallen god.

Some days,
trees are just trees,
mud is mud.

The Green

What could be so surprising about a bowling green
on Sydney's cliff-top outskirts, when that same stretch

hems a spacious cemetery, the path to heaven
topped off by a five-star view of sapphire sea?

But the green – such an English scene – grass shaved
to a suede finish. So much patience required for bowls.

I bet it's not Australians who created this. They run
where they can walk, surf where they can swim,

whereas my father's idea of a walk was to stroll
across a bowling green, its calm smoothing the creases

of his soul, and he tried to persuade my brother to find peace
the same way, my brother who had rarely known calm.

The day Dad died, Paul and I walked to the green.
My Dad's died, he wailed over and over, *My Dad's died*.

He cried as he delivered the news to strangers,
cried unrestrained so that, bowls poised, men paused.

A life had stopped. A man's son was here to honour him,
noisily. Only the green remained undisturbed.

Cicada Love Song

Like lads who congregate in squares
of French or Spanish villages, like men
grouped at a table outside an Italian bar,
you and the cicada boys hang out
to flex your tymbals and flick your wings,
build your trance and techno buzz
to rev up any female for a mile around.

Hot pink hibiscus, bougainvillea –
and yours the persistent soundtrack
to all our lazy holidays. The hotter the sun,
the louder the stridulation, your vibrations
the escalating thrum of how it was
to be young, thirst never quenched,
heat like a hungry kiss on the skin.

At the Juliet House, Verona

You can buy a heart. Plastic,
sealed with a seam. It'll sit
in your palm, unbeating.

You can rub the bronze of Juliet's
right breast, wish for a new love
to come to you within a year.

You can stand on the balcony
in blue shorts or a wedding dress
and call your Romeo's name.

But the balcony was carved
from an old sarcophagus
for a Hollywood film of the play.

And history shows no Juliet –
although, if you write to her
at this address, Juliet will answer.

Late, Alone

It's late, you're in bed. I suddenly miss you.
Alone with a jug of dead flowers, I miss you.

I look at the stars and shiver, glance
at the unlit fire and I miss you.

There were days, four counties apart,
I'd do nothing for hours but miss you.

I see us still, curled in a single bed
under the tartan rug, and I miss you.

Some day two will be one. I freeze
to think of all the ways I would miss you.

I say to myself, Girl, where have you been?
Go to him now and say it: *I miss you.*

I'm Probably Wasting My Time and Yours

I waste my time pulling off the black jeans
and putting on the blue jeans.
I waste my time taking off the blue jeans
and pulling on the leggings.
I remove the leggings and replace them
with the black jeans. I waste my time
half listening to news on the radio
while reading news on my phone.
All morning I'm wondering who
was the sputtering man on *Today*
and what was his point. When I fret about
the stuff I always fret about,
you cut across me with the same frustration
I feel over wasting time.
I waste time staring from my window,
hoping an axe will relieve my neighbour's tree
of its excess height and give me back
my green-shouldered hills.
I waste time reading emails lauding
hotels I'll never visit, shoes I'll never wear,
storage solutions for a slovenly house.
Despite all the time I spend signing petitions,
hospitals fall sicker and sicker, the planet burns,
That Man is still at large, unmodified.
I waste time on educational documentaries,
during which I fall asleep. I waste time
watching *Pointless*. Unbelievable
how much time I waste looking for lost objects,
excavating the many zip-up compartments
of my handbag, attempting to recall the location

of that safe place. There is no safe place, what's lost is never coming back, what's done cannot be undone. Say something, please.

I'm on Page 3

of the piece about Plath's Bee Poems,
a feminist analysis. He walks in,
looks at the computer screen,
asks me to come and hold the ladder.

I know he will do the job
whether I help him or not.
The chainsaw, the wobbly ladder:
no threat will stop him from acting *now*.

I leave my room, follow him out.
I steady the ladder, he wields the saw,
while my head fills
with an insistent, furious buzzing.

when was ecstasy

some nights the moon is so big
i almost remember ecstasy

the body raised to a chant of joy
the soul woken and shaken

*

frost-cold out there
no bird no human or animal call

wind's held breath – then a bus
lists silently down Stoke Hill

*

floating in the night sky
beyond the bedroom window

a man with two profiles
is reading in bed

*

we snuffle under winter covers
like the garden table and chairs
asleep in their plastic overcoats

the trampoline lies redundant
where are the jumping boys?
where is summer?

*

there were times
when joy pinned wings on my back
when ecstasy claimed me

come with me to the mountain top
when day is new

come with me and stand astonished –
if just for a moment

Black Cat and Rabbit

In the middle of my tale about Nita, how I am paralysed
by her rage, how she leaves me nowhere to go,
how love and pain sit hand in hand with her,
I see through the long glass garden doors, your cat
come from the field, pantherish in sleek all-black,
with his luxuriant stroll. He's bringing you
a grey rabbit, limp in his jaws, its neck in his mouth,
paws dangling. It must be dead. But dropped on its side,
among the wallflowers and forget-me-nots, the rabbit
scrabbles, legs running and running to raise itself.
It can't get up, but works to survive, while the cat
observes. You are saying we're stuck, Nita and me,
in a cycle of attack and freeze, freeze and attack.
I start to answer but break off. I can't not watch
what's happening outside. The cat's paw shoots out
and again the rabbit jerks. *Please let it stop.*
Then Richard appears with a spade and I look away.

Tales of the Poets

He said, It's okay to write shite;
    in fact, it's essential.
He said, Poems about animals are good,
    especially when
they are not really about animals.
    He said, When Ted Hughes
wrote about a salmon, he was really
    writing about himself.
Surprise yourself! he said. You have to watch
    how an animal moves,
notice it ten times more exactly than a non- writer.

He told us, William Carlos Williams was a doctor
    and wrote poems
in the minutes between seeing one patient
    and the next.
Elizabeth Bishop pegged her poems on a line
    in the kitchen
to amend while she was cooking.

I noticed, during his reading, he sometimes
    SHOUTED VERY LOUDLY,
WHILE EYEBALLING HIS AUDIENCE,
    a kind of poetry Ian Paisley.
Genius. Those sleeping woke up.
    The rest of us
relieved the tension by laughing.

Since we met, I have taken the poet's advice,
    writing many pages of shite –
some about animals.
    Any time soon, I'm sure
I'll surprise myself.

on not being william carlos williams

i wish i was the kind who could be content
with a wheelbarrow in a yard

i would look out from the breakfast table
at the garden i'd no doubt have if i was that type of person –

the organic vegetable patch, the rows of sweet peas & homunculus
a word i think i've heard in connection with flowers –

& dash off poems
in miniature
about the wheelbarrow

its colour and shape
the glorious sheen
from the rain

but i'm not that easily inspired
when it comes to
garden implements

as for the yard
i could sit in the sun
& consider my homunculus

or the wheelbarrow
i do not own
& did not want

till i brought it to my attention

The Nearly Times

Once, when a group of horses bolted
and reared, eyes white, legs flailing,
trampling whatever was under their hooves.

Once, wheeling too fast on a bike
down Richmond Hill, tumbling off. Stilled
on the tarmac, a human speed bump.

Once, when a guy drove us into a lamp-post.
Chin gashed, hand crushed, broken wrist.
Soon healed, though I still have the scars.

Mostly I've been careful, or lucky, or both,
but once I pulled out in the path of another car
and once clipped the side of a thundering truck.

I bless Sheldon Kaplan, who invented the EpiPen.
Once I passed out at a party and wasn't drunk.
Everything went dark. I was blind till I honked.

How many lives is that? How many chances,
how many years was I handed to learn
how to live every day, how to give thanks?

The Waves

You say the city pavements are choppy
with ice. Snow spits at your face, flies
at huddles of the homeless. Alone
in the building long after midnight,
you try to calm the stranger with Jesus hair
just two steps away from you. He plunges
hands in his pockets to feel for something
hidden. You know tonight, again,
you will not sleep. Everyone is sinking,
everyone signed off sooner or later.
Sometimes you call in sick, but only when
you talk about drowning is anyone
nervous enough to listen. So you tell them
about the waves, how sometimes
one rears up high as a house. They say
if you can't stay afloat, get out of the water,
let someone else do the job. And you look
at the gentle faces on the poster on the wall;
you look out of the window at Rosanne,
nineteen, half-naked, trying to suck warmth
from a roll-up; you look at the closed door
of the manager's face, the wave suspended,
high over your head. You can feel
your face breaking, imagine walking out,
picking your way over the treacherous ice
on a one-way trek through the city.
Then, with an inward breath, you think again
of that bus driver yesterday, who stopped,
climbed out of his cab, to help
a blind man in a swirling sea of traffic.

Acknowledgments

Some of these poems, or versions of them, have appeared in the following journals: *The North, The Rialto, And Other Poems, Obsessed with Pipework, Ink Sweat & Tears,* and *Snakeskin.*

'Young Again' features in *The Listening Walk* anthology (Bath Poetry Café).

'The Waves' won Second Prize in The 2013 Yeovil Literary Festival Competition and in the 2019 Poetry Business and Wordsworth Trust Single Poem Prize.

'Cicada Love Song' came out of a workshop with Fiona Benson and was selected as one of the audio poems on Exeter University's Arts and Culture site: www.artsandcultureexeter.co.uk/arts-commission/fiona-benson-2020-arts-commission/output

Many thanks to Annie Fisher, Liz Barnes, Paul Tobin and Sue Norton for their always perceptive comments and to Peter Sansom and The Poetry Business for making this publication possible.